The Birthday of Guru Nanak

Festivals Around the World

©2017
Book Life
King's Lynn
Norfolk PE30 4LS

ISBN: 978-1-78637-031-0

Written by:
Grace Jones

Edited by:
Charlie Ogden

Designed by:
Matt Rumbelow

The Birthday of Guru Nanak

Festivals Around the World

Hello, my name is Ajeet.

When you see Ajeet, he will tell you how to say a word.

What is a Festival?

A festival takes place when people come together to celebrate a special event or time of the year. Some festivals last for only one day and others can go on for many months.

Some people celebrate festivals by having a party with their family and friends. Others celebrate by holding special events, performing dances or playing music.

What is Sikhism?

Sikhism is a **religion** that began over five hundred years ago in India. **Sikhs** believe in one God, whom they pray to in a **gurdwara** or Sikh place of **worship**.

A gurdwara in Delhi, India.

Ajeet says:
GURD-VAR-A (Gurdwara)
GOO-ROO GRANTH SY-YEEB
(Guru Granth Sahib)

Sikhs follow the teachings of their gurus or holy teachers. They instruct people on how to practise their **faith**. Sikhs also read a holy book, called the **Guru Granth Sahib**, which guides them on how to follow their religion.

Who is Guru Nanak?

Guru Nanak is a very important person in Sikhism as he started the Sikh religion over five hundred years ago. Guru Nanak taught people that there is one God who is always with us, wherever we are.

GURU NANAK

How do Sikhs Celebrate His Birthday?

Sikhs celebrate the birthday of Guru Nanak in November of every year. During the festival people hold large street parades, go to a gurdwara to pray and eat special food with their family and friends.

Gurdwara

The birthday of Guru Nanak is celebrated for up to three days.

The Story of Guru Nanak

A long, long time ago, there once was a man called Guru Nanak. One day, just after he had celebrated his thirtieth birthday, Guru Nanak disappeared for three days.

When he reappeared, he began to practise the Sikh faith and spent the rest of his life spreading the word of God to others.

GURU NANAK

He taught people that everyone was equal, no matter whether they are rich or poor, a man or a woman, or if they followed a different religion. This is still one of the main beliefs of Sikhism.

Guru Granth Sahib

The Guru Granth Sahib is the Sikh holy book. It was written by a group of Sikh Gurus who lived over four hundred years ago. Copies are kept in a special place protected by a hanging cloth in the gurdwara.

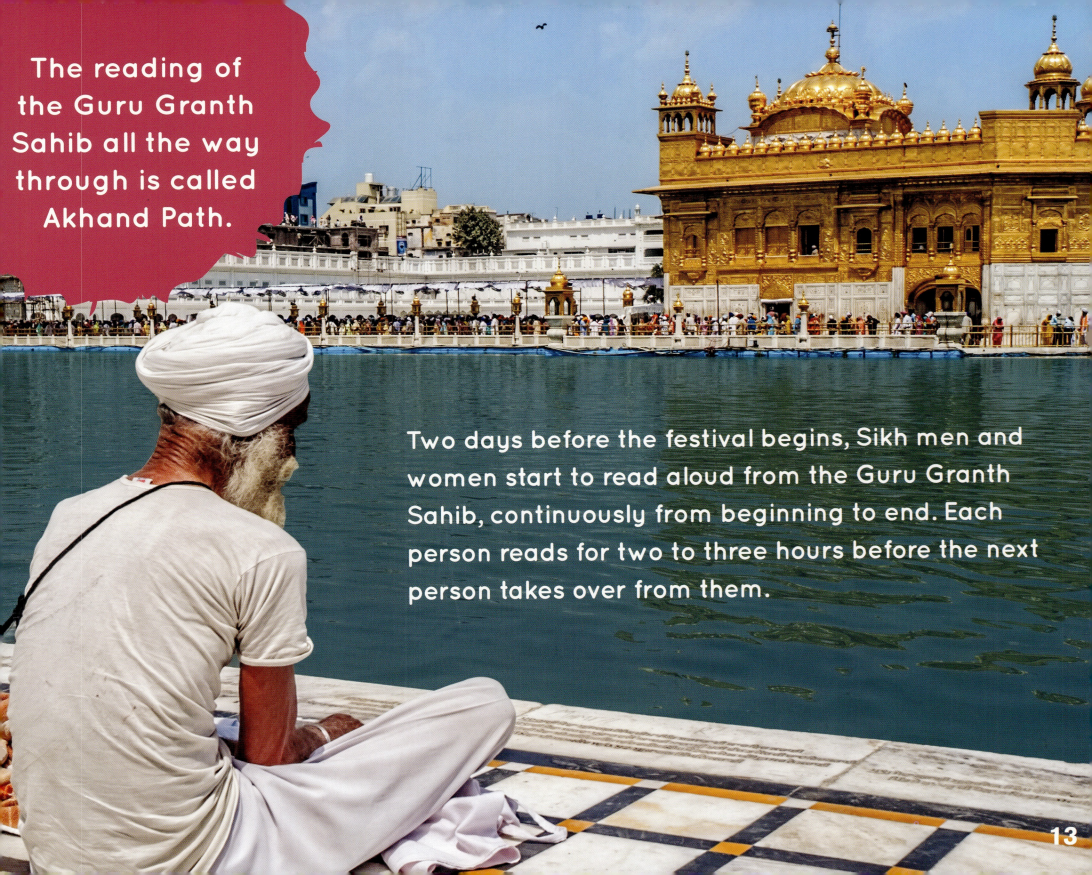

The reading of the Guru Granth Sahib all the way through is called Akhand Path.

Two days before the festival begins, Sikh men and women start to read aloud from the Guru Granth Sahib, continuously from beginning to end. Each person reads for two to three hours before the next person takes over from them.

Celebration Parades

To celebrate Guru Nanak, Sikhs parade through the streets. They are led by five men who represent the **Five Beloved Ones** or Panj Pyare and they carry the Sikh flag. These men are very important in Sikh history because of their commitment to the Sikh faith and its teachings.

The parades are called Nagar Kirtan.

They are followed by teams of many singers and musicians who sing hymns and play different tunes. Streets and houses are often decorated with banners, flags and flowers for this special occasion.

Ajeet says:

NAR-GAR CUR-TAN (Nagar Kirtan)
PANJ PEE-ARE-REE (Panj Pyare)

Prayer and Worship

On the morning of the festival, celebrations begin when the sun rises. Sikhs travel to a gurdwara to pray, sing hymns from the Guru Granth Sahib and share stories about Guru Nanak's life and beliefs.

Sikhs who cannot visit a gurdwara during the festival hold prayers and tell stories in their homes.

Festive Food

After prayers, a sweet food, called **Karah Parshad**, is blessed and eaten at the gurdwara. It is made from wheat flour, sugar and butter.

KARAH PARSHAD

Ajeet says:

CAR-AH PAR-SHAD (Karah Parshad)

LUN-GAR (Langar)

Everyone then shares a free meal together, called a **langar**. Only **vegetarian** food is served so that everyone can eat together.

Family and Community

The birthday of Guru Nanak is a time when Sikhs celebrate their faith and remember the Guru who started their religion many years ago.

It is also a time to share with one another and spend time with your family, friends and community.

Ajeet Says...

Gurdwara

"GURD-VAR-A"

A Sikh place of worship.

Guru Granth Sahib

"GOO-ROO GRANTH SY-YEEB"

The Sikh holy book.

Karah Parshad

"CAR-AH PAR-SHAD"

A sweet dish made from
wheat flour, sugar and butter.

Langar
"LUN-GAR"
A shared meal which takes place at a gurdwara.

Nagar Kirtan
"NAR-GAR CUR-TAN"
A Sikh parade where hymns are sung.

Panj Pyare
"PANJ PEE-ARE-REE"
Another name for the Five Beloved Ones.

Glossary

faith great trust in someone or something

Five Beloved Ones important Sikh men who were extremely faithful to the Sikh religion

religion a set of beliefs based around a god or gods

Sikhs people who follow the Sikh religion

vegetarian a person who does not eat meat or fish

worship a religious act, such as praying

Index

Credits

Photocredits: Abbreviations: l-left, r-right, b-bottom, t-top, c-centre, m-middle.

Front Cover: l; India Picture, r; India Picture, bg; szefei. 2 - India Picture, 4 - Tom Wang, 5 - India Picture, 6 – saiko3p, 7 - Tukaram Karve, 8 – szefei, 9 – saiko3p, 10 – szefei, 11bg – 302988455, 12l – saiko3p 12r – Curioso, 13 - OPIS Zagreb, 14 - Sergei Bachlakov, 15 - India Picture, 16 - Pius Lee, 17 - Luciano Mortula, 18bg - India Picture, 19 - Tukaram Karve, 20 – 220407958, 21 - India Picture.

Images are courtesy of Shutterstock.com. With thanks to Getty Images, Thinkstock Photo and iStockphoto.